Dear Paul,

Lovely to meet you,

Mending The Ordinary

Liz Lefroy

Liz x.   WPF 2016

For Helen Lucas

This collection was first published in Great Britain by Fair Acre Press in May 2014

Typeset and Cover Design by Nadia Kingsley

Printed by Badger Print, Sutton Maddock, Shropshire

© Liz Lefroy 2014

The right of Liz Lefroy to be identified as author of this work has been asserted in accordance with Section 77 of the Copyright, Designs and Patents Act 1988. No part of this book may be used or reproduced in any manner whatsoever without written permission by the Publisher except in the case of brief quotations embodied in critical articles and reviews

A CIP record for this book is available from the British Library

The author thanks the editors of *Magma*, *Writers' Hub*, *Mslexia*, and *The Writing Room* where some of the poems were first published

Midwinter Moon is dedicated to Ryan Kennedy, at Radio Shropshire. *Snapshots* is dedicated to Sally Lefroy (1937-1989)

Born in London, Liz Lefroy lives in Shrewsbury and works as a lecturer in social care. Liz won the 2011 Roy Fisher Prize for new work in poetry, resulting in the publication of her first pamphlet, *Pretending the Weather*. This was followed in 2012 by her sequence, *The Gathering*. Both were published by Long Face Press.

ISBN 978-0-9568275-7-9   www.fairacrepress.co.uk

Contents

3	In The Queue In The Waitrose Café, I Meet My Love			
4	My Son, Playing Bach		15	The School Concert
5	Outlet Village		16	Waiting For Oblivion, At Alton Towers
6	Grace		17	Returning After A Holiday
7	Solving Insomnia		18	The Path
8	Question Answer		19	Always The First Day
9	Durham Cathedral		20	Grandfather Clock
10	My Ambiguous Relationship With Rain		21	I dreamt you were trapped
11	East Lambrook		22	This Is The Printable Version
12	Snapshots		23	Is
14	Midwinter Moon		24	The Square Root Of Paradise

In The Queue In The Waitrose Café, I Meet My Love

The man next to me in the queue is gorgeous.
It starts with him telling me I've dropped my pen
and I pick it up, though it's not mine.
I'm almost sure he knew that anyway
so we talk about pens and dropping things.
I ask for a cappuccino and we're on to poetry.
While the milk is frothed, he says for him
it's about what sounds like daffodils.
I tell him about my rhyming dictionary.
He says, *So, you're a clever girl then!*
I smile, say, *No*, then, *Yes*, to chocolate.
We laugh as I hand over a five pound note.
If I were fifty years younger I'd fall in love with you.

He says this as I hold out my hand for change.
All this in minutes, and I already love him.
He's eighty-five, but I won't believe it.
He looks at me from the corner of his eye,
gives a nod of knowing, asks for two cups of tea,
hooks his stick over his arm to pay.
I say, *Lovely to meet you,* walk to a table
past a woman who is smaller than him,
creased into a chair and wearing pink socks.
I look up at them from time to time.
I see their silence. It's been a long time.
It's just been a long, long time.

My Son, Playing Bach

Downstairs my son is playing the piano
square on, as it were, to the music.

It was made for his long fingers,
for this particular touch, and he is careless with it

as if stopping were of no consequence.
No need, for now, to perfect the cadence.

For him, tomorrow holds no silences -
only this music, and all its beginnings.

Outlet Village

Less a place than an occupation: an attitude
against our empty Sunday afternoon, this squat
mock-timbered, park-out-of-town thronged
by faces set in sparse light and spits of northern rain.
It's not beautiful, cannot redeem itself with bargains
- a change of linen, a watch, another pair of shoes -
or stuffed ciabatta and bottles of coke consumed
between blasts of heat felt at each shop entrance.

But when my son, taller than me now, says,
We're shopping under cloud-light,
I feel the world unlock. We turn
to each other, laughing
and alive. The sky is water,
limitless. And we're swimming in it.

Grace

Today we played Frisbee on the beach.
You weren't there. I skimmed it to you anyway
knowing you would catch it firm in your palm
or spinning on the tip of your finger.

When it was my turn I dropped it.
Everybody laughed, but you gave me
excuses to play with - a sudden lift of wind,
an unexpected flight.

Solving Insomnia

Some nights when I cannot sleep
I set myself in the tall house
grey-built from Kentish rag-stone
which stands next to the church.
I let myself in with the key I've kept
and tiptoe up avoiding the dog
and the fifth stair of the third flight
so as not to wake my parents.

In the room with one red wall to warm it
I pick my way across discarded toys,
settle into the bed under the eaves.
My brother lies next door
propped on one hand reading
Biggles Flies Again.
Below, my solid father snores.
I face west, fall into the old dreams …

… of tomorrow, when my mother will sing
as she makes a picnic which includes
crisps, Mars Bars and orange squash.
We will go to the open air pool
where I will break the record
for fifty lengths and dive like a mermaid
drawing attention from my brother's friend
and the casting agent of a new film.

I will lower my head demurely
when the Queen asks me to the palace,
an invitation which requires me to have a dress
that is white with a blue sash.
The dog will have a miracle of puppies
and I will name them again and again:
Cholmondeley, Olly, Jessie, Holly and Moss.
I will count them, count them.

Question

In answer

to your question -

which is not

a solitary thing

though it has

the appearance

of a soft landing

falling as if

from a branch -

in answer

to your question

I will try to think

of what it is

you think because I

like you and if you are

like me you'll desire

the security of echo

of hearing yourself

repeated to emphasise

your point.

That's straightforward enough isn't it?

Answer

As I said at the time

It depends.

Durham Cathedral

Years on I return, park, walk through slant rain

to see the west end looming from the wooded bank.

I didn't know 'til now that I'd hoped to see something

collapsed, something ruined with the quality of Rievaulx

which frames far more than it ever held.

These towers have stood too long - can I say that?

I want this shrine to have risen up, stood

medieval, then, weeping with the flow of history,

seeped its grain into the Wear's loop,

the living stones a testament

to how I find things mostly are:

swift, growing, stumbled - yielded to the weather.

My Ambiguous Relationship With Rain

The last time I wet myself
I was tending my rabbits in the rain.
I couldn't leave them, couldn't not go,
so pissed myself as I passed them
ripped up grass through the bars.

And halfway across Europe my father
steered us through a downpour,
though the week before we'd spent our words
petitioning God for good weather.

I mourn the rich-rained green of the garden.
The hostas drip from their chewed tips,
and the roses rot brown on their stems.
But my son, who is not afraid of rain,
who refuses to carry coat or umbrella,
comes home, wet and strong.

East Lambrook

Velvet curtains drape against the rain   warm chairs crowd round a fire   the clock
plucks slow time   You're reading   I'm sitting   album on my knees   your mother's

leaning in   pointing out your childhood   Each photo's a place within this place
of love   I recognise the white-framed squares   greenish now

     wet costumes on a tiny beach   your dog caught in a cuddle
               an eccentric line of relatives
     three children on a tractor   a picnic on rugs on heather   you in plaits school uniform
     five children strung out along a cliff path heather
                  you amidst the games on a lawn mown for childhood

You're there   I'm here copying handstands   paddling in your pool   contesting
the rules of French cricket   chalking hopscotch on your granny's path

I recognise those boys   their brown Startrite sandals   I know about running   tumbling
grass down necks   about egg sandwiches   lemonade   chocolate cake

Under the table our grass-stained legs swinging in unison

Snapshots

My first day at school;
you, leaving me in suspense,
lessen the goodbye
with a sugared promise.
Later, we walk home,
and in my other hand
a cake crumbles in relief.

You sit down, offering
the sanctuary of your lap.
And up I scramble.

Highbury sweats under
the summer of parched earth.
Daytime, I peer into the cracks,
seeking your Antipodean dream.
At night, under the eaves,
my hot feet twist sheets
into fretfulness.

Christmases wake to the weight
of your love wrapped
into a rustling stocking.
And the rush to you
for the opening of secrets
right down to the orange.

It is summer, a day out,
I think you are happy.
As we pass the kiosk man he says
you are far too young.
I am proud because
you catch attention and throw it off
so easily.

We lean forwards,
eager to be the first to see
the finger of Salisbury's spire
pointing to the freedom
of the white steps, which lead
to water and our buoyancy.
And all of us re-wrapped
in your mother's noiseless love.

Your brother's unruly arrival
loosens our home
into the exhilaration
of its two pianos.
Together, you present to us
The Queen of Sheba
in brilliant handfuls.

I cannot remember
the actors' names, what they said,
the other girls, whether we ate ice cream.
But I can see you waiting
in your long coat,
lit somehow.

Once, you let us find you
stripped down to your tears;
holding out hands which had
propped up the world you cry:
*Look! Loneliness also mingles
with love.* We turn from shame,
and a silence coming between us.

You know, you say,
I might die.
In my shocked suspense, you reach
for that other hand, placing it
on your hardened breast.

Midwinter Moon

This moon is far-fetched:

the thinnest of crescents frosted

into a deep sky.   It's perfect

as a story: I expect shepherds

and starlight as a minimum,

though I don't need them

to announce themselves

as miracles.   It's enough

to go out in it, hear the crunch

and give of frozen ground

underfoot, stretch my arms up

through the bare trees,

open my mouth
                        to receive

the season's sacrament:

the first flakes of snow on my tongue.

The School Concert

Son, you don't know this but last night
at the concert I disgraced you by exploding.
It was when you sat, back straight,
intent at the piano and all my love for you
crescendoed into beats so loud they surely
drowned out your perfect notes.
I shut my eyes, controlled my breathing
as at your birth.
                        It was as useless
as it was then and my life burst out of me,
flooded the hall red with all the years
since our final strain of childbirth.
Last night they applauded you
as they should have done then, when,
open-mouthed, you sang cries to the new world.

Waiting For Oblivion, At Alton Towers

Six minutes into One Hour's Wait From Here
we're shifting our feet and I'm thinking up strategies,
rooting through my bag for anything that'll subtract time
from nothing to do but creep forward with the rest of them.

It's a change from the hurtle, yet no less challenging,
this ebb in the flow of adolescence: queuing for a ride
that'll scare me stupid for the sake of being with these
way-past-the-minimum-height boys of mine a little longer.

They are leaning on the ropes, casual, more than ready
for this pounce on adulthood. They've discussed it,
set hearts on talking about it to anyone who'll listen,
tweeting a moment as imperative as a coming of age.

It'll age me too, the feeling I'll have that I've had before:
my stomach rising through the roof of my head
as I'm strapped into the point of no return, ratcheted up to the edge
of the plummet, where I'll hesitate, rigid, before the fall.

Returning After A Holiday

Two weeks away, and when I return it's dark.
I leave my case in the hall, hang up my coat,
take off my shoes, go through the sleeping house.

I remember this lock, the way the key needs to sit
just *so* for the levers to give and turn.

I step out into the intended scent of sweet peas
and onto dry twigs, meaning the pigeons
have built their careless nests nearby.

It must've rained here for things not to have died,
for them to be knee and shoulder high.

The grass is like this: a deep coolness held in itself
so to lie on it is obvious, to press my face down
into the feel of what must be green.

I sense the long tap of the rose on my back,
bending under its low weight of petals,
reminding me to turn over, to look at the stars.

The Path

It was a well-packed week.
By this I mean I carried what I could –
a tent, some clothes, one book,
plasters for emergencies,
money folded small.

I recollected myself.
By this I mean I left the splits of life –
dusty work, tired affectations,
the shuddering life of buildings,
fridges and desires.

I lived as I wanted.
By this I mean I tended my needs,
went about the early things,
ate an apple with my bread,
washed under a tap.

I made no judgements.
By this I mean I saw the sea's purpose
below the rocky cliff-fall,
felt the warmth and retreat
of the sun's widest arc.

I walked with myself.
By this I mean I met others
face on, always in advance,
greeting them softly
with a nod, a smile.

I saw the wind's power.
By this I mean I watched full sails
glide across sea-blue skies,
clouds surge up beyond
the gull's curved flight.

I slept without dreams.
By this I mean I found by evening
my body was at peace,
worn by its uses,
bedded down on clean earth.

Always The First Day

It's time to go upstairs,
take off the usual things.
I empty my pockets of keys, tissues,
that shopping list, a bill, fluff.

I unzip my jeans,
pull my jumper over my head.
I holiday naked – it's the only way –
lying flat on a wide white bed
in this room growing bright from the sea.

And it's always the first day, the day
with the stretch of everything
unfurled through the open windows
to a crisp horizon cut with sails.

Grandfather Clock

In the stairwell of the house where everything belonged to God
the grandfather clock leaned forward on uneven boards.

Its whirring mechanism, familiar as the swift uptake
of my father's staggered breath before a sneeze,

pre-empted the tones and blasts of hours which accompanied
those perpetual years and days in which I grew.

I learned to wind the heavy cylinders just far enough,
was reconciled to each mark and numeral of its old face.

Lying upstairs between the striking hours of vacant nights
I knew panic at the mounting loss of sleep towards school,

but here I began the sufficient learning: how to endure
the space between tick and tock, between word and word,

between what the word says and how the world goes,
between each week's winding, each moment's gradual fall.

I dreamt you were trapped

burning the school burning though it was not your school but a hall
and you were in the hall beyond and I was calling calling your name

dark-haired boys streamed from my focal point out past my peripheral vision

but not you

I woke filled with smoke
and going about dressing   going about breakfast was uneasy

I didn't phone did later left a message feeling the fever
of love the way it anticipates the fall scrape   bruise cut break

the burn

the way it marshals its matchstick fleet of words
careful! steady! look out!

it'll be all right

21

This Is The Printable Version

This is the printable version
and it involves lying down again.
I lie still on my bed, wearing everything,
even my shoes, and wait for sleep.
I will not think for a while.

For now, the residual warmth,
its leaking benefit -
avoidance, stillness -
blankets me.

My mother would say,
If you keep your coat on,
when you go outside
you won't feel the benefit,
though I never found this to be true.

I wonder,
did you?

Is

rain against the window and the beat of it is

the patter of fingers on a drum skin is

the breeze so much softer than the coolness is

breath on my face, the longing for sea is

thought of current and its traces in the sand is

as glassy as the look of ripples underfoot is

where I sat with my legs stretched out to the west is

how I sat with my legs on the glassy white sand is

waves on my legs on the ridged white sand is

the waves sucking out and the waves running in is

underneath the wave before the running out to sea is

the wave turning round its own far reaches is

the break of the wave, the broken green wave is

broken and made and broken and made is

the making and the breaking of the words that I say is

words like the waves and the thought of them now is

keys tapping words against the clear bright glass is

my fingers tapping keys like rain on the glass is

the beat of the rain like the letters that I type is

the words reading me from behind solid glass is

words drumming light between your eye and this page is   is   is   is

The Square Root Of Paradise

Reduce it all to this? The number of a god?

The number of gods? The numbers of gods

divided up and into themselves?

There are thousands of ways to be improbable.

Can anything as immeasurable as glory

be balanced like an equation?

Paradise is a salvage operation,

a reckoning of what we desire stretched,

unbroken, from here to infinity,

like syrup twisted onto a spoon, lifted up high,

tipped to a skeining - a long stitch of sweetness

mending the ordinary.